Ella,

Happy Christmas

Love

Ger & Carol.

2018

# What if ?

by Sarah Murphy

f What If? Sarah Murphy

For my husband Andrew who encouraged me, for my sons Dylan (thanks for the ball on the road idea) and Shane (thanks for the cover idea).

For my friend Mary Salmon who supplied the buffalo idea and great feedback. For my family, and the memory of my parents Sean and Ethna Murphy and for their wisdom.

Many thanks also to the children in Gaelscoil Na Dúglaise, Cork for their suggestions.

What if you could eat all the sweets in the world!?

your tummy would not thank you ...
just a few might be better for you ____

What if your football rolled out onto the road?
That's my new ball.
oh no!

but you faced the fear and it disappeared!
what if the dark were ⬤ or ⬤ ?

What if somebody makes a mistake in a test?

2 + 3 =

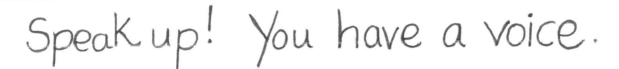

. . . if you get a bad feeling say "no☺"

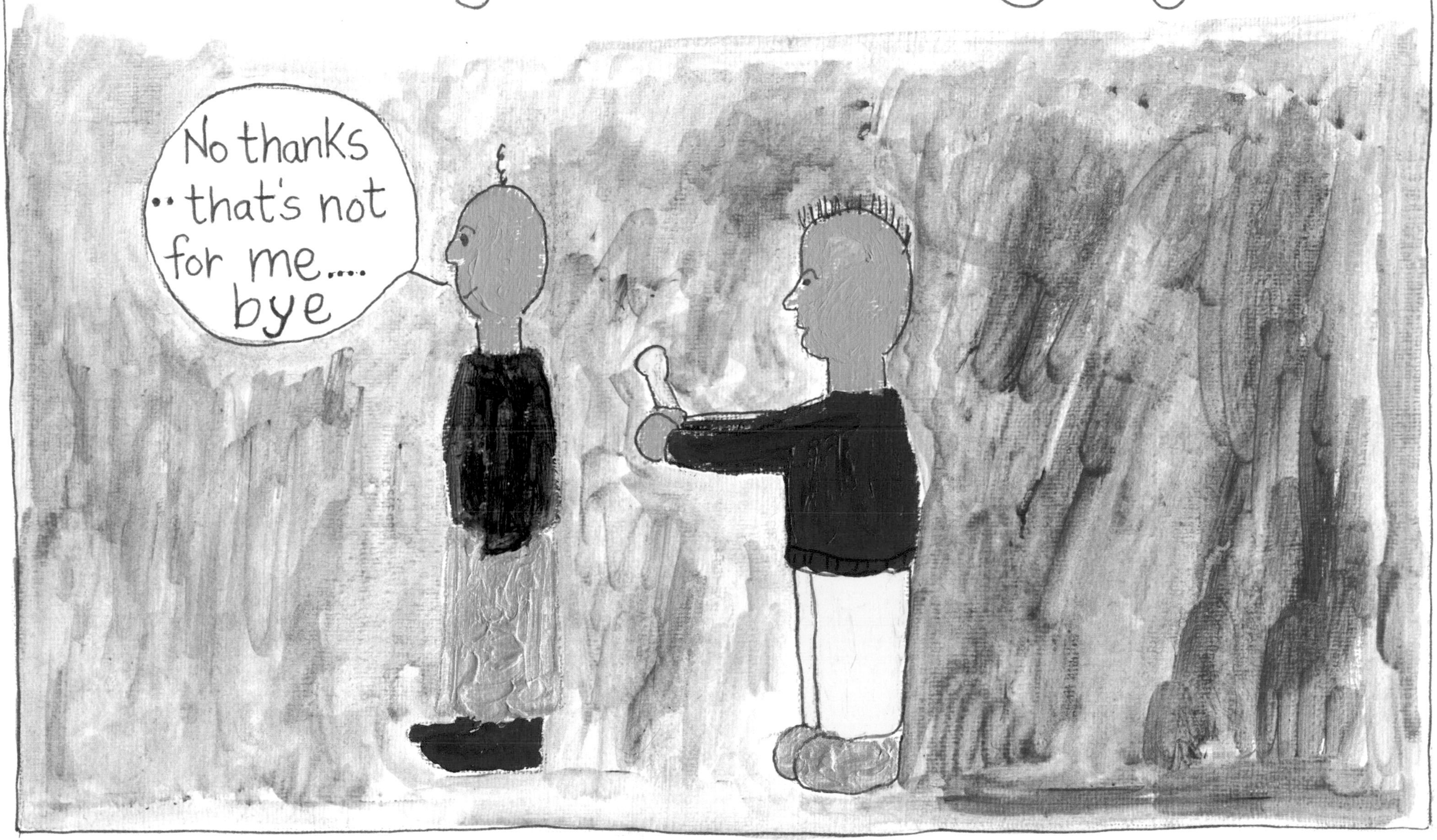

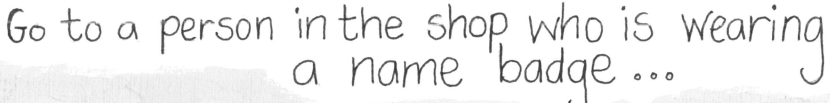

What if you broke the window when playing
ball?

Sarah age 5. I didn't win the cup! My Dad woke me up one night to have my photo taken with this rugby cup.

When I grew up I became a Montessori Teacher and later on an Art Therapist.